totally relaxed

totally relaxed

techniques to create calm in mind, body & soul

Emily Clayton

THUNDER BAY
P · R · E · S · S
San Diego, California

THUNDER BAY
P·R·E·S·S

Thunder Bay Press
An imprint of the Advantage Publishers Group
5880 Oberlin Drive, San Diego, CA 92121-4794
www.thunderbaybooks.com

Copyright © Salamander Books Ltd, 2003

A member of **Chrysalis** Books plc

All notations of errors or omissions should be addressed to
Thunder Bay Press, Editorial Department, at the above address. All other correspondence
(author inquiries, permissions) concerning the content of this book should be addressed to
Salamander Books Ltd, 8 Blenheim Court, Brewery Road, London, N7 9NY, U.K.

ISBN 1-57145-958-8
Library of Congress Cataloging-in-Publication Data available upon request.

Printed in China
1 2 3 4 5   07 06 05 04 03

CREDITS

EDITOR: Marie Clayton
DESIGNER: Claire Graham
PRODUCTION: Don Campaniello
COLOR REPRODUCTION: Anorax
PRINTED AND BOUND IN CHINA

Contents

Introduction

Life can be very stressful, and to deal with it effectively on a day-to-day basis we need to know how to relax at the right time and allow our worries to drift away. Relaxation allows us to bring things back into perspective and bestows the welcome gift of peace to a troubled mind. If you are not able to relax, the stress can quickly build up until it becomes unbearable.

Unfortunately, being able to relax when we need to is not a gift that comes naturally to many of us—it is something that we may need to learn. To be totally relaxed, we need to be able to let go in mind, body, and spirit. However, bringing calm into your life can be relatively easy if you regularly follow a few simple exercises, techniques, and tips.

The way we breathe is one of the most powerful tools we have to calm both mind and body. If you can learn to breathe slowly and rhythmically, really focusing on each breath, you will soon find that tension begins to flow away. Start your day with a sense of balance and control by choosing one of the five-minute meditations featured in this book. Gentle exercise regimes, such as Pilates, yoga, chi gung, and tai chi, can ground and balance you, helping to generate a firm

base from which you can move forward into the day.

A feeling of self-worth is an important part of being able to relax properly. If we are not really sure of our own identity, it causes conflict that will soon spill over into every area of our lives. Learning to accept yourself for who you are will give you a wonderful feeling of inner peace. When you can avoid giving negative opinions of yourself to others—or even just to yourself—then you will soon begin to feel a change. Learning to write and say your own affirmations each day will quickly boost your feelings of self-worth and motivate positive changes in your life.

Exercise itself can be a very important part of the relaxation process. Even something as simple as a brisk walk will reduce tension and tendencies to depression, and change your conscious thoughts. For those who find it difficult to remain still, walking with awareness is an ideal form of moving meditation.

The use of essential oils and flower essences is a gentle, relaxing, and very efficient way to reduce tension and stress. When you are out and about and do not have good access to other means of relaxation, they can provide an ideal emergency treatment. Learning which is the best oil or essence for each situation will help you use these powerful tools in the most effective way. Each will work best when used in a specific way—they can either be added to the water at bath time, used in a carrier oil during massage, or dropped on pulse points for a quick and effective tonic.

The gift of inner contentment and peace is a wonderful feeling that everybody should be able to enjoy at will when they need or want to. Not all the strategies for relaxation shown in this book will work for you, but somewhere in these pages is the ideal relaxation technique that will transform the rest of your life.

CHAPTER ONE

Stress: The Twentieth-Century Affliction

In prehistoric times when people lived in caves, the appearance of a predator triggered a rush of adrenaline to fuel a "fight or flight" response. Now we live in a different world and the threats that we face are as likely to be chemical or emotional as they are to be physical—but our bodies react in the same way. Without a physical response to use up the adrenaline, situations can cause anxiety and tension, leading to physical illnesses such as raised blood pressure.

Some stress is good—it motivates us into action—and the good feeling we get after a job well done is a form of stress. Without it we would have no stimulus or motivation, and life would become very boring.

Assessing your stress levels is relatively easy—there are certain life events that will generate "good" or "bad" stress in all of us. When your stress reaches a certain level, it is time to take action to avoid future problems.

Attitude is also an important factor—viewing what happens as a threat generates negative stress, but if you can look on your life's events as challenges or opportunities, they will generate positive stress instead.

ASSESSING YOUR STRESS LEVEL

There are certain events in life that will cause stress.
A number of them are listed opposite and on the following
pages, along with a "stress value." If your personal score over
the last twelve months comes to more than 150, you are
suffering from stress—if it is over 300, the stress
could be affecting your health.

LIFE EVENT	STRESS VALUE
Death of a life partner	100
Divorce	80
Marital separation	75
Prison term	70
Death of a close family member	70
Personal injury or illness	60
Marriage	55
Loss of a job	50
Marital reconciliation	45
Retirement	45
Ill health of a family member	40
Pregnancy	40

LIFE EVENT	STRESS VALUE
Change in financial state	40
Death of a close friend	40
Change in job	40
Child leaving home	35
Arrival of new family member	35
Outstanding achievement	30
Moving home	30
Vacation	25
Christmas	25
Other major holiday	25
Minor law violation	20

GOOD STRESS

BAD STRESS

POSITIVE STRESS

is stimulating, and you

feel refreshed and

pleased afterward.

NEGATIVE STRESS

causes anxiety and tension,

and you feel drained and

depressed afterward.

23

As well as life events, other things in our
environment can cause stress, including physical
factors, chemical toxins, and electromagnetic waves.

PHYSICAL STRESS INDUCERS

Allergens

Toxins

Temperature extremes

Injury

Poor light conditions

Enforced inactivity

CHEMICAL STRESS INDUCERS

Alcohol

Caffeine

Nicotine

Sugar

Poor nutrition

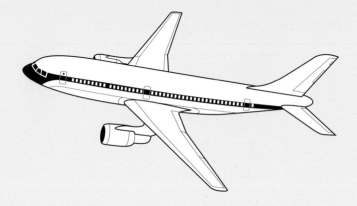

ELECTROMAGNETIC STRESS INDUCERS

High-power electricity cables

Cellular phone signal masts

Computers

Fluorescent lighting

Television

Airplanes

We are responsible for our own attitudes and behavior. You can regard unpleasant events as setbacks and become upset about them—or you can regard them as challenges that will help you grow and develop new ways of coping with your problems.

Be positive.

When life gives you lemons...

Make lemonade.

THE SYMPTOMS OF STRESS

PHYSICAL SYMPTOMS OF STRESS

Back, shoulder, or neck pain

Breathing problems

Dizziness

Frequent minor illness

Headaches

Heartburn

High or low blood pressure

Nausea

EMOTIONAL SYMPTOMS OF STRESS

Depression

Fatigue

Indecisiveness

Irritability

Lack of concentration

Nervous exhaustion

Stress does not have
to rule our lives. Take
action and
take control.

Learning to relax
is the key.

41

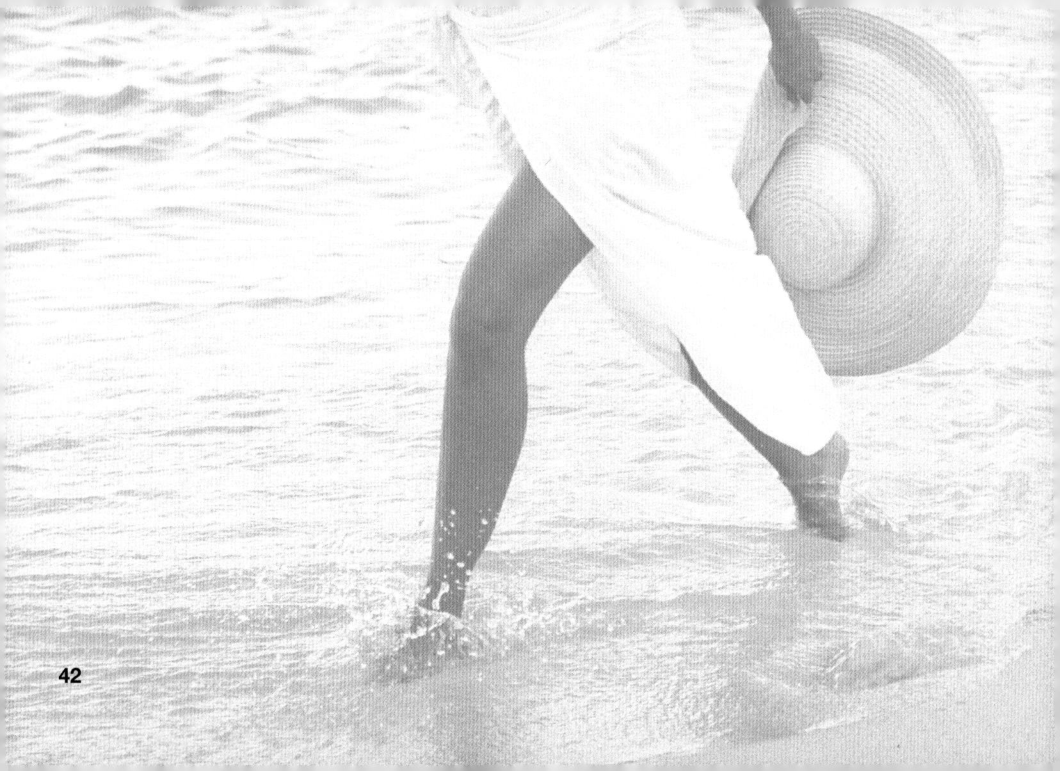

CHAPTER TWO

The Power of Relaxation

It has been scientifically demonstrated that at least eighty percent of all psychosomatic illnesses can be controlled by regular deep relaxation. Taking at least thirty minutes of proper relaxation a day will balance blood pressure, regulate the pulse, and moderate any other stress symptoms. If you can achieve twenty minutes of deep relaxation twice a day, it will reduce both your adrenaline production and your insulin requirement by at least fifty percent over a twenty-four-hour period.

Deep relaxation involves more than just sitting down. You need to be able to relax your whole body and your mind at the same time, but by using a few simple techniques this is quite easy to achieve. Learning to breathe correctly, using visualization techniques, and exercising regularly will all help speed the process and allow you to relax at will.

Although it will certainly be beneficial to set aside specific times for deep relaxation each day, there is also much to be gained by relaxing for a few moments at any time. Taking a few minutes off to consciously relax during the working day will enable you to return to your tasks fresh and alert, and prevent stress from starting to build up.

Being healthy is a natural way of life—but the majority of illnesses are the result of lifestyle choices, and stress is a major cause of disease. Stress levels are significantly reduced by relaxing regularly.

Relax

and change your life.

There are many ways to relax, and some that work well for you may not work for others, and vice versa. Try several techniques until you find one that you enjoy and that works for you.

At least thirty minutes of relaxation a day is the minimum you should be aiming for, but you can build up to this over a period of time. As you begin to relax, you will feel so much better that it will be much easier to proceed.

5

TOP FIVE RELAXATION TECHNIQUES

Deep breathing

Meditation

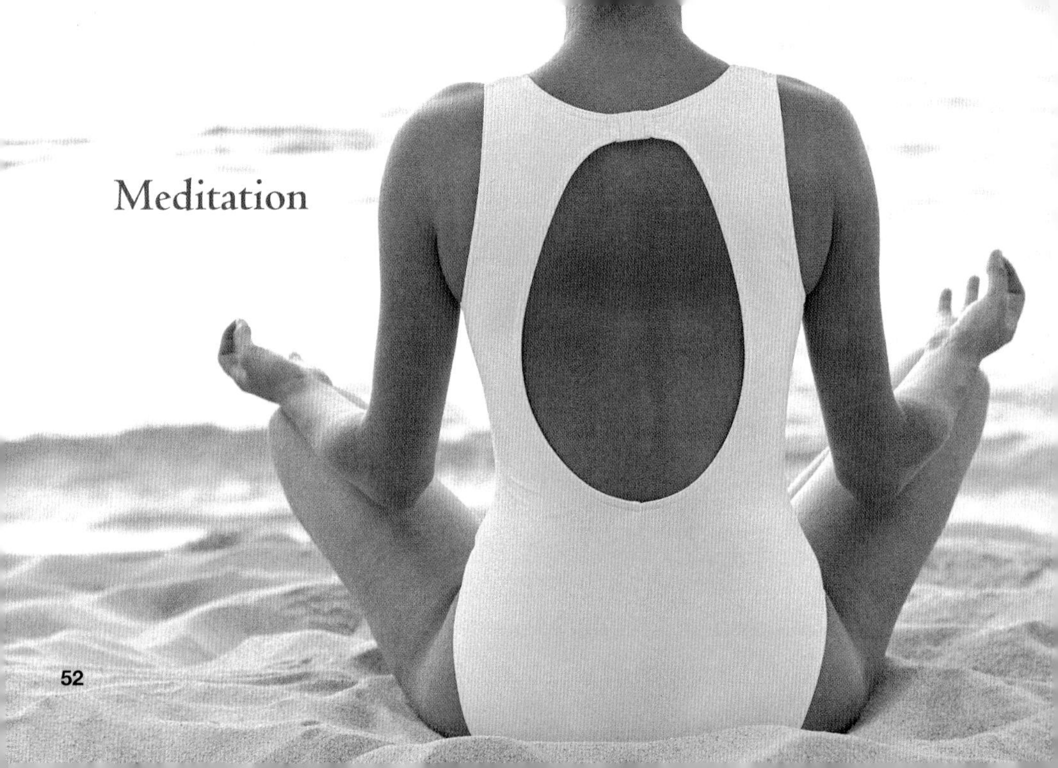

Listening to a relaxation tape

Taking a long,
soothing bath

The mind-body link

The power of our minds has a great effect on our bodies, but in many cases we are unaware of the connection. You can learn to understand your body properly by doing a few simple exercises.

Talk to your body.

Tell yourself you feel *warm*.

After about twenty minutes you will

begin to feel *warm*

USE VISUALIZATION

Imagine lying on a beach with the sun beating
down on your body until it begins to
warm in the sun's rays.

Concentrate on one part of your body.

Tell yourself that your hand feels relaxed.

Tense up the muscles in that area, then release.

Do this twice, then feel the area relax.

Be aware of your heartbeat.
Listen to your heart. Imagine it slowing into
a calm and regular beat and it will gradually
start to slow down.

BODY BREATHING

Imagine you are breathing through the skin of your hand. Concentrate on the breath in and out of that area for at least twenty minutes, and you will find it becomes numb. As you become more adept, this can become a good method of controlling pain in any area of the body.

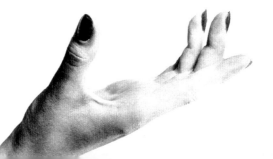

Once you have learned to consciously control your body with your mind, you will be able to use the same techniques in reverse, moderating your body's physical reactions to control your emotions

Top tips to
relax at work

Take time to go for a ten-minute walk at lunchtime.

Move away from your workplace to eat lunch.

Cut down intake of caffeine and other stimulants.

Sit still and take eight deep breaths when your stress level rises.

Take a few moments to "be" in the middle of doing.

Accept that you cannot do everything.

CHAPTER THREE

Creative Visualization

Creative visualization involves seeing events clearly in your imagination as you would wish them to be. If you do this over and over again you will be feeding this imagined data into your subconscious, until your mind accepts it as reality. The problem for many of us is that we are constantly visualizing very successfully—but using negative thoughts instead of positive ones! Filling your mind with thoughts of failure will inevitably cause you to fail.

The key to making visualization work is to develop a positive scenario for any future event that is worrying you and to continually rehearse mind. If any negative options come to you, develop a positive strategy to deal with them—and then accept that this is how it will happen.

As you keep repeating these positive thoughts, you will be forearmed to deal with any eventuality—and you will have faced the situation in advance in a positive way. This will greatly reduce any anxiety caused by anticipation, since you have already planned how to deal with the situation in your mind. Creative visualization is one of the simplest ways to banish worry and achieve equanimity.

Using visualization techniques means you are
taking a positive role in creating your own future.
By changing your mental attitude you can change
a negative reaction into a positive one.

When you feel you have no
control over a given situation, panic
attacks can often happen. If you
are in control, there is no
need to panic.

If you are someone who worries a lot, you are already able to visualize really well—the problem is that you are visualizing negative scenarios rather than positive ones.

All you have to do is turn your talent around and make it work for you instead of against you.

When facing an event that worries you, start by imagining all possible scenarios, from the best to the worst. If you are realistic when imagining the worst-case scenario, you will already have faced up to the worst that can happen—and survived. You can then move forward to work on more positive outcomes.

Practice regularly by concentrating on something that you find pleasant. This will make you more positive as a person—and therefore more able to take advantage of any opportunities that may come your way.

Just before going to sleep, practice relaxation techniques and then begin imagining what will happen the following day, making sure that everything goes as you would like.

Remember that you are in control, so you can make everything perfect. If any negative thoughts do occur, put them aside.

"*It's only a thought and a thought can be changed.*"

Louise L. Hay   *You Can Heal Your Life*

A few visualization
exercises

You can also use visualization to
relax, to get rid of unpleasant emotions,
and to diminish pain.

If you are feeling angry or upset, imagine
your bad feelings growing wings and then
watch them fly away.

If you are feeling stressed, imagine walking along a beautiful beach in the sunshine— feel the sand between your toes.

If you are feeling pain, visualize what shape and color the pain is, then imagine it dissolving away.

If you have problems fantasizing
scenarios, use pleasant memories from
your past instead. Happy thoughts lift
the emotions and alter the body's
chemistry in a positive way.

Use visualization to find a place
of peace, change the way you react to
the world, find inner security, and
create a secure future.

CHAPTER FOUR

Behavioral Patterns

The way we behave conditions how people behave toward us and so the way in which our lives progress. Everybody has patterns of behavior that they repeat over and over again—some good, some not so good. Sometimes it may not be so easy for us to see which is which—what we see in ourselves as confidence and self-assurance may be seen by others as being pushy and self-centered! Before deciding to make any changes in your behavior, it is a good idea to look at yourself honestly—but also to ask close friends to be honest about how they see you as well. You may find that what you feel is "bad" and needs changing, they regard as part of your charm—in which case the answer is to accept and make friends with yourself the way you are.

Part of our behavior is conditioned by events in our past, but we can learn to release these memories and let them go. Some patterns of behavior can cause us harm, by leading to stress, obsessive actions, or panic attacks. If you can learn to step back, identify these patterns, and take an objective look at what triggers such behavior, it is much easier to prevent it from happening again.

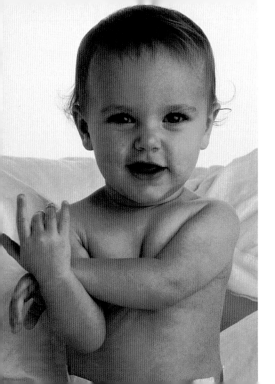

Babies do not have to do anything to be perfect.

They are born without bad habits and hang-ups.
We pick up bad emotional baggage on our way
through life—but we can just as easily choose
to put it down again.

The past cannot be changed—
but the future will be shaped
by our current thinking.

When we have some habit deeply ingrained within us, we have to become aware of it before it can be changed.

Every habit we have is there to fulfill a need within us. If you can establish what caused the need and deal with it, the habit will no longer be necessary.

Take a pad and pen and write
"I SHOULD" in large letters across the top.
Now come up with six different ways that
you can finish the sentence.

When you have your six things you feel
you "should" do, write next to each of them the
reason why *you should do it.*

Finally, write down the reason in each case why you have not done what you "should" do.

The last answer will probably be very revealing—you

may have been angry with yourself for years for not doing something

you didn't want to do in the first place! Or for something that you were

only trying to do to please someone else. Now that you know that you did

not want to do these things, you can drop them from your list of

things that you want to achieve.

You only have to meet
your own standards in life—not
everyone else's as well.

If you can learn to love yourself, your own standards will be realistic and achievable—and you will have a sense of satisfaction in meeting them.

Many people believe they cannot enjoy life today because of something that happened in the past. If you write down your reasons, they will often strike you as being fairly silly right away.

Because my love left me, I can no longer be open to love.

Because I did not get that promotion, I will never succeed.

Because I was hurt then, I will never trust again.

Because I was poor as a child, I will never have any money.

Perhaps the people who hurt you in the past
were not aware of the fact—and today they probably
don't really care, either. By hanging on to your bitterness and
resentment, you are not hurting them—only yourself.

If you can truly forgive those who have hurt you, the bad feelings will dissolve and you can move forward with your life.

Think of what you were wearing when you were six. You wouldn't wear the same clothes today—however much you loved them then, you don't feel the same way about them now—they are just a memory. So why are you hanging on to the past and wearing outmoded feelings?

Feelings from the past are no longer relevant today—

just as clothes from then are no longer fashionable.

You need to let go of the anger and forgive.

*Imagine that someone
who has done you wrong is
standing in front of you.*

In your mind, do not direct resentment at them, but wish them all the good things in life, see them smiling and happy... then watch them slowly fade away, taking your anger with them.

Bitterness and
resentment keep
you pinned down
in the past.

Forgiveness and acceptance allow you to move forward into the future.

Loving ourselves is the key to banishing many problems. The cure is simple—but surprisingly difficult to put into action effectively.

Sit in front of a mirror and look

yourself straight in the eyes. Tell yourself:

"I love you, and I accept you as you are."

Persevere until you can do it.

CHAPTER FIVE

Meditation:
Discovering the Quiet Within

Meditation is one of the simplest ways to relax and to allow the stress in your life to flow away naturally. It not only leads to mental peace and serenity, it also tunes the mind so that it functions much more efficiently. It is not complicated—it involves sitting silently and focusing on one object or sound, allowing the mind to empty all extraneous thoughts, so that both mind and body relax completely. However, like many such simple-sounding processes, this can often be very difficult to achieve successfully without a great deal of practice. At first, the constant activity of the mind will be difficult to slow down, with stray thoughts constantly breaking through and interrupting your concentration.

Different meditation techniques work for different people, so if one method does not work for you, try another until you find one that does. However, practice is the key, so you should try to set aside a specific time every day. It does not have to be a very long period—better a short time that you can manage on a regular basis, than a longer period that is difficult to fit into your daily schedule. As you begin to feel the benefits, you will be motivated to find more time.

Where to meditate

Quiet places are better than noisy ones.

Some light is ideal—total darkness is not recommended.

A place where you will not be disturbed.

Comfortable temperature—not too hot or too cold.

Somewhere where you can make yourself comfortable.

Try to use the same place, so that going there will

begin to trigger the right frame of mind.

When to meditate

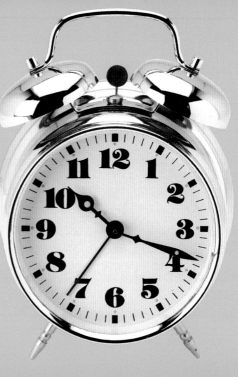

Choose a regular time each day.

Early morning, early evening, or before bed is ideal.

Start with 15–20 minutes a day.

Build up to 30–60 minutes a day.

Rituals are not essential,
but will help to get you into the
correct frame of mind.

Wear dark or neutral clothing.

Sit in a comfortable position.

Light incense or a candle.

Start and end the session by

sounding a bell.

Starting to meditate

After getting into a comfortable position, focus your attention by counting your breaths.

Count one as you inhale.
Count two as you exhale.

Your counting should be inaudible.
Do not try to control your breathing—
even if it feels too shallow or too fast.
Continue counting until you reach
ten, then begin again.

At first, you will almost certainly find
that stray thoughts will interrupt your
concentration. Notice they are there, but do not allow
them to dominate your conscious mind and they
will soon float away again.

If intrusive thoughts have made you lose count, just begin again at one.

If difficult issues arise, you may chose to deal with them by letting them run their course. As you become more experienced at meditating, you will be able to accept and release inner conflicts before returning to counting your breathing again.

With practice, you may experience heightened awareness while meditating, and enjoy feeling a lost harmony *between body and soul.*

"*I take care of my own life—I take care of the world as my own life—moment by moment, and in each situation I enable the flower of my life to bloom...*"

Kosho Uchiyama *Opening the Hand of Thought*

If you find it difficult to concentrate on your breathing, you can try focusing on something else instead, such as a lighted candle.

Use the **candle** technique in the evening. Light it and settle down comfortably in front of it. Look at the **candle** flame from about three feet away for five minutes, then blow it out and close your eyes.

You will be able to see the afterimage
of the **candle** flame in the middle of
your forehead. After a few seconds it will
begin to fade away—but if you concentrate
you can bring it back and hold it
in your mind.

sound

Another technique is to use sound instead,
focusing on a single word, sound, or phrase.

Although you will need
to create conditions that are
as close to ideal as possible
when you first begin meditating,
with practice you will be able
to meditate for short periods,
even under adverse conditions
if necessary.

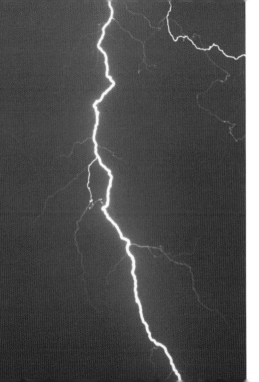

Deep meditation is the experience of being totally at peace, no matter what is happening outside. With practice, you can withdraw your concentration totally from your external senses and focus inward.

CHAPTER SIX

Breath of the Soul

Deep breathing is one of the quickest and simplest ways of relieving stress quickly and relaxing the body gently. Taking deep breaths increases the amount of oxygen in the body, which eases tension and improves circulation. Most of us spend much of our lives breathing shallowly and failing to use the full capacity of our lungs. Learning to breathe correctly not only reduces stress, but over time it will also increase your energy and help you to sleep better. Correct breathing also aids correct posture—the two work together in perfect harmony as the body comes into alignment with itself.

Many Buddhist traditions focus on the act of breathing as a basis for meditation. Everyone knows how to breathe—it is a process so natural that we can forget we are doing it—but concentrating on breathing in and out regularly without being distracted by every passing thought can be immensely difficult—it can take a great deal of time to get it right. There are also several other breathing exercises you can try, all of which will help you focus and relax. Approached the right way, breathing will soon become an important factor in your relaxation program.

Deep, unforced breathing is achieved when the diaphragm and chest muscles work together in harmony, and it can give you a new feeling about yourself. Deep breathing is also one of the quickest and most effective ways to relax.

When you are stressed, your breathing will become much shallower and faster, which makes the blood more alkaline and can lead to hyperventilation and panic attacks. If you realize this is happening, you can quickly reverse the process by taking slower and deeper breaths.

Begin by getting into a
comfortable sitting position,
but keep your back straight
and your spine extended.
Keep your chin level, stretch
your neck up and forward,
and look straight ahead.

Exhale slowly through
both nostrils. As you reach
the end of the out breath, pull
your stomach in and hold
for one second.

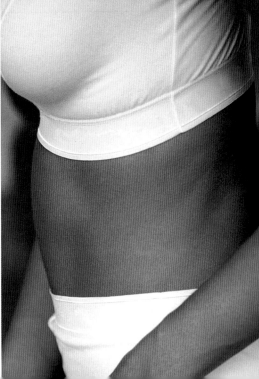

Inhale as deeply as possible, feeling the air enter your abdomen first, then fill your chest, then fill the top of your lungs. As you breathe in, imagine a wave of energy traveling up from your abdomen to your forehead. Hold in the breath for one second before exhaling.

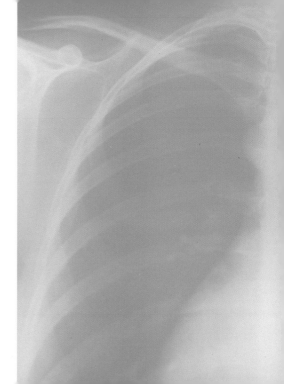

Every cell in the body needs a constant supply of oxygen, so the ability to breathe fully and freely is very important.

If you normally breathe using your upper chest muscles rather than your diaphragm, you are not using the full capacity of your lungs and your body is not getting a full change of air.

How do you breathe...

Sit in a chair with arms in front of a mirror.

Breathe in deeply and see if your shoulders rise—

if they do, you are an upper-chest breather.

To correct upper-chest breathing and learn
to use your diaphragm correctly, sit with your arms
on the chair armrests and push down with your forearms
and elbows as you inhale. This will prevent you
from using the wrong muscles.

Repeat the exercise ten times, exhaling for
six to eight seconds and inhaling for two to three seconds.
Try to do the complete exercise at least twice a day. You
do not have to set aside a special time or place—you
can even do it at your desk.

If you fail to push air deep into your lungs, where the gaseous exchanges your body needs take place, you will lose too much carbon dioxide. A reserve of carbon dioxide is just as necessary to your body as taking in fresh oxygen.

In really bad cases, a depleted level of carbon dioxide will lead to hyperventilation, causing dizziness, palpitations, tingling in body extremities, and sometimes chest pains.

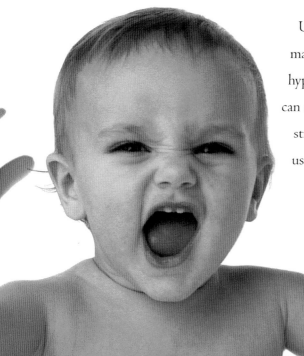

Upper-chest breathing will make you more susceptible to hyperventilation, but an attack can also be triggered by excessive stress—because stress causes us to breathe more shallowly.

During hyperventilation attacks, the automatic response is to feel you are not getting enough oxygen—so you breathe faster and even less deeply. In fact, the reverse is true—you need to breathe slower and deeper to top off your reserves of carbon dioxide.

To stop an acute attack, breathe in and out of a paper bag to reestablish the acid-alkaline balance.

Sit straight, but relaxed, with one hand to your face,
so you can use the thumb to block one nostril and
a finger to block the other.

Close your left nostril, breathe in, and count to three. Close the right nostril, exhale through the left nostril, and count to six. Breathe in again through the left nostril. Repeat alternately for ten rounds.

CHAPTER SEVEN

Mind Power

The mind is far more powerful than any other factor in defining how our life is shaped. We create our own experiences by our thoughts and our feelings. We create all the situations we find ourselves in, and then often feel powerless to deal with them. In truth, since we are creating our own reality, we can also learn to change it. If we can create peace, harmony, and balance in our minds, we will find it in our lives.

What we believe about ourselves and our lives will come true, because our subconscious will accept what we choose to believe and automatically react accordingly. If you believe people are helpful to you, the way you approach them will encourage them to help. If you approach them feeling they are out to get you, your air of mistrust will tend to keep them at bay.

This does not mean that you should start to blame yourself for what is going wrong in your life, because that is reacting in a negative way. Each of us does the best they can with the tools at hand, but with the knowledge of how to create a different reality, you can move forward in a positive way.

"Every thought we think is creating our future."

Louise Hay *You Can Heal Your Life*

If you had one friend who constantly criticized you and another who was always positive about your good points—who would be the most pleasant to spend time with?

You are your own best friend—
so be nice to yourself.

Looking at negative thoughts

Make a list of all the bad characteristics you believe you have.

Look at each in turn—is it really true?

Who told you it was true?

Most of the negative thoughts we have about ourselves come from our childhood—someone has told you that you were bad at something and now you believe it yourself—so it has become true! But things change. You may have found it difficult to do something when you were a child, but maybe you were just not ready then.

Deciding to change

To change your negative thoughts you have to be willing to change. You need to move from positive to negative. Remember it is all in your head—you are in control.

Resentment, criticism, and guilt are damaging emotions.
Banish them from your mind to achieve inner peace.
Every time you think a negative thought, turn it
around so it becomes positive.
Don't say "I want," as that is only a wish—
say "I have" or "I am."

NEGATIVE

"I want to lose weight."

"I am afraid of doing that."

"I hate my job."

POSITIVE

"I am losing weight."

"I am confident and fearless."

"I am going to find a wonderful new job."

"The power of positive thoughts and actions leads to fulfillment and happiness and defends the body against illness by keeping it balanced."

Uri Geller *Mind Medicine*

Set your goals.

Make a list of what you would like to achieve. Start with where you plan to end up—where you would like to be in a few years' time.

Then list your midstage goals—
where you need to be to get halfway
to where you are heading. For
instance, if your long-term goal is
a career change, perhaps your
midterm goal would be to
start the training for your new
career, or taking a job where you
can start learning more about
what it involves.

Finally, you need to set your short-term goals—what you need to do next to start making all this happen. There is no need to make giant changes all at once—beginning with small changes can make a difference as long as they are taking you in the right direction.

"A journey of a thousand miles begins with a single step."

Stay focused—when you are focused
on where you are going, you can visualize a
positive outcome and this will help you
make it through any setbacks.

But also allow yourself the freedom to change your mind about what you want to achieve as you move along and new vistas open up.

Life happens—but you can choose
how you will react to external factors.

Sometimes there are things we cannot change, however **positive** we might try to be. It is then important to learn **acceptance**. Without acceptance, you will not achieve **peace** of mind.

The happiest people in the world are those who have recognized that life is not perfect, and that they alone are responsible for their own happiness.

CHAPTER EIGHT

Heal the Body, Heal the Mind

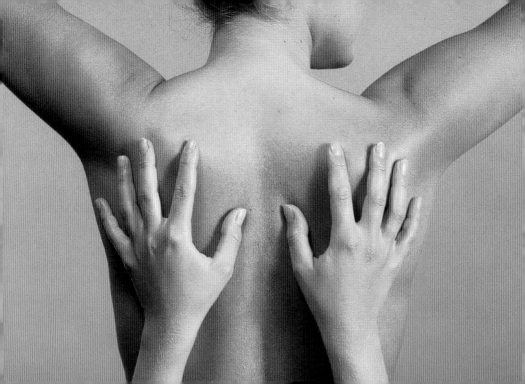

Just as we can use the power of the mind to relax the body, we can also use the body to relax and quiet the mind. One of the more powerful physical ways to relax is by using different forms of massage.

Massage is one of the oldest and simplest medical treatments, although in the West it has only recently become accepted for its wider health benefits. It can be stimulating or soothing, depending on the speed and depth of the stokes, and can relieve tension, soothe headaches, relax muscles, and induce a sense of well-being.

Essentially, massage is an extension of something we often do automatically—we rub painful areas and stroke distressed children to soothe them. Even stroking a household pet is a form of massage, which has been proved to lower blood pressure and have a relaxing effect—both on you and the pet.

There are several different massage techniques, but most are fairly easy to learn. The simplest form of massage relaxes the muscles, ligaments, and tendons to relieve tension, but more complicated techniques, such as shiatsu and reflexology, can be used to unblock energy paths and realign the entire body.

PREPARATION

The person receiving the massage should be comfortable. Choose a room where you will be undisturbed and make sure the temperature is comfortable. Massage can be given on the floor or on a table, but pad hard surfaces with plenty of towels. Do not massage on a spring mattress, as it will absorb all the pressure.

You will need to oil each part of the body as you start to work on it, so your hands will slide over the contours without friction. It will also nourish the skin.

Ready-made massage oils are often expensive.

You can also use vegetable oils such as sunflower or coconut.

Almond oil is pleasant—but expensive.

Baby oils are suitable, but may be less easily absorbed.

Keep your oil in a corked or flip-top bottle.

If you are giving an aromatherapy massage, add

a few drops of essential oil to your basic oil base.

Make sure the oil is comfortably warm
and rub it between your hands before
applying. Only a thin film of oil is needed,
but since it is quickly absorbed by the body,
only oil each part as you get ready to work
on it. The oil is applied and rubbed
in with long, gliding strokes.

Making and breaking contact with
the body should be done gently and
with sensitivity. Make sure your hands are
relaxed as they touch the body. Some
experts recommend always keeping
one hand in contact with the body,
but this can be difficult to do as
you move around.

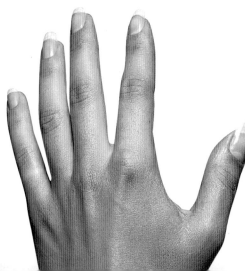

Basic strokes

LONG STROKE

A gentle, rhythmic stroke in which your hands glide
over the skin. It is used on all parts of the body to apply oil
and to warm and relax the area.

BROAD CIRCLING

This stroke also serves to spread the oil over the skin.
Move the hands in fairly wide circles, each overlapping
the previous one as you move along the body to
form a continuous spiral pattern.

FEATHERING

Lightly brush the skin with
your fingertips, using
your hands alternately. This
stroke is mainly used to break
contact with the body gradually.

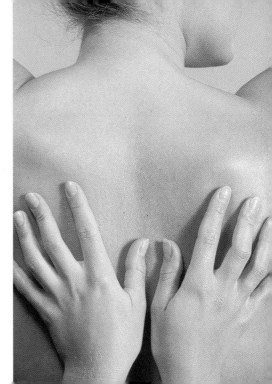

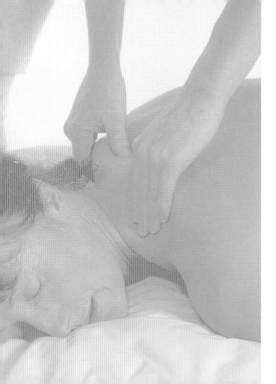

KNEADING

This is used to stretch and relax the soft, fleshy areas of the body. Using your whole hand, grasp and squeeze a handful of flesh. As one hand releases, the other gathers a new handful. Work smoothly down the body as if you were kneading dough.

WRINGING

In this stroke, the hands move toward each other from opposite sides of the body, so the flesh is first bunched up and then stretched between them. Place your left hand on the near side of the body, heel down, and your right hand on the far side, fingers down. Push forward firmly with your left hand and pull back with your right until they have swapped positions on the body. Without stopping, change directions and keep going in a continuous, flowing motion.

HEEL OF HAND PUSHING

Push the heels of your hands gently but firmly
into the flesh, bringing one down just behind the other.
Move your hands alternately and rhythmically.

THUMB ROLLING
Press the balls of your thumbs
away from you into the flesh,
using short, deep strokes or
small circles.

HACKING

Using relaxed hands, place them about three inches
apart with the palms facing one another and the sides resting
just above the body. Bounce the sides of your hands alternately
and rapidly, up and down on the body.

PUMMELING

Loosely clench your fists and bounce your hands
alternately up and down. The motion should be firm,
but fairly light.

CUPPING

Cup the palms of your hands but keep the fingers fairly straight. Repeat the same alternate drumming sequence as in pummelling. The cup of your hand will trap air against the skin, making a sucking sound.

PLUCKING

Pluck or pinch small amounts of flesh between your thumb and fingertips, using alternate hands.

Sequence of working

Back of the body, working from head to feet.

Work over the whole area, then concentrate on specific places.

Back of the legs, working up and then down.

Moving to the front of the body, work on shoulders, neck, and scalp.

Face, starting on the forehead and working outward from the center.

Arms and hands, working up and then down again.
Front of torso, starting on the rib cage, around
the abdomen, and up the belly.
Front of legs, again working up and then down.
Finally, link all the parts of the body, using long strokes or by
resting your hands briefly on two separate parts.

As well as relaxing the muscles,
a full massage will boost lymph
and blood circulation, the
nervous system, and the body's
flow of energy.

238

CHAPTER NINE

Aromatherapy for Body and Soul

Aromatherapy is the technique of using the scent of essential oils to heal the mind, body, and spirit. These essential oils are the pure extract from herbs, flowers, and resins—the oil is held in tiny sacs on all parts of the plant. In their concentrated state they are extremely powerful, so they should always be used in very tiny amounts, added in drops to the bath, or diluted in a neutral carrier oil for use during massage. Drops of undiluted oil can also be used in a perfume burner, to cleanse and energize an entire room.

The use of essential oils goes far back in history—the ancient Egyptians used them in religious rites, and in beauty preparations to increase the elasticity of the skin. As well as improving our bodies, they also influence our moods and behavior. Different oils have different properties—some of them are stimulating and some are relaxing, so it is important to know which is the right one for the job.

The oils used in aromatherapy retain the characteristic aroma of the plant they come from and their rich scent is integral to the healing process. It is important to use good-quality oils, so they should be bought from a reputable source.

Never swallow any undiluted
essential oil. The leaves of some
plants and herbs can be made
into infusions or herbal teas, but the
undiluted oil is far too strong.

Always measure out the quantity carefully—
some are highly toxic in larger amounts.

Never apply undiluted oils
directly to the skin.
For massage, body moisturizers,
and beauty treatments, add a few
drops to a carrier oil.
For bathing and room sprays,
add to water.

Store essential oils in a dark, airtight bottle and keep cool and out of sunlight.

The oil will need twenty-four
hours to penetrate the skin
fully, so do not bathe or take
a shower immediately after
an aromatherapy massage.

SOME OILS CAN CAUSE SKIN IRRITATION—CONSULT
A DOCTOR IF THIS OCCURS.

The following oils should not be used during pregnancy:
angelica, basil, fennel, juniper, laurel, marjoram,
rosemary, tarragon, thyme, yarrow

CONSULT A DOCTOR BEFORE TRYING ANY ESSENTIAL OIL
OR TREATMENT WHEN PREGNANT.

Smell is a powerful sense that can affect your emotions, evoke memories, and even cause a physical response. They can *relax* or *stimulate*

Different oils are appropriate for different circumstances.

Energizing

Geranium

Ginger

Jasmine

Myrrh

Neroli

Pine

Bergamot

Chamomile

Geranium

Jasmine

Lavender

Easing stress

Marjoram

Neroli

Orange

Rose

Sandalwood

251

Bergamot
Lavender
Lemon
Marjoram
Neroli
Orange
Patchouli
Sandalwood
Tea tree

Soothing anxiety

Aiding sleep

Chamomile

Cypress

Geranium

Lavender

Lemon

Neroli

Rose

Ylang-ylang

Easing fatigue

Cypress
Eucalyptus
Ginger
Lavender
Orange
Peppermint
Rosemary
Rosewood

Lifting depression

Bergamot
Frankincense
Geranium
Lavender
Orange
Rosemary
Rosewood
Sandalwood
Ylang-ylang

BERGAMOT
Light, sweet, fruity scent
Light green color

CHAMOMILE
A calming oil with a fresh scent
and herbaceous undertones
Light blue or clear pale
yellow when fresh, turns darker
yellow with age

CYPRESS

Fresh, woody, balsamic scent

Greenish-yellow color

EUCALYPTUS

Herby, camphorous,

medicinal scent

Dark yellow color

FRANKINCENSE

Rich, warm, balsamic scent

Pale yellow to greenish in color

GERANIUM

Sweet, strong, lively, floral scent

Yellow to olive-green color

GINGER

Spicy, lively scent

Pale yellow color

LAVENDER

Flowery, fresh, slightly

medicinal scent

Clear color

LEMON

Lively citrus scent

Pale yellow color with a
greenish tint

MARJORAM

Warm, spicy, floral,
herbaceous scent

Clear to pale amber color

MYRRH

Smoky, bitter, slightly
musty scent

Dark reddish-brown color

NEROLI

Fresh, spicy, bitter, floral scent

Pale yellow color

ORANGE

Sweet and lively, fruity scent

Dark yellow to orange color

PINE

Aromatic, balsamic scent

Colorless to pale yellow

ROSE

Delicate, sweet, floral scent

Dark to pale yellow color

ROSEMARY

Refreshing, herby scent with

woody undertones

Clear color

ROSEWOOD

Sweet, spicy, floral, and
slightly woody scent
Clear to pale yellow color

SANDALWOOD

Sweet, woody, balsamic scent
Pale yellow to clear color

TEA TREE

Strong, fresh, medicinal scent

Pale yellow color

YLANG-YLANG

Heady, floral scent

Yellow color

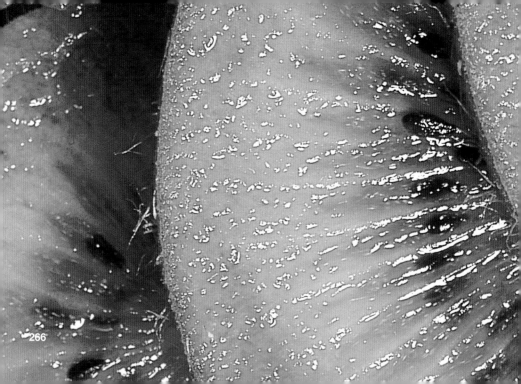
266

CHAPTER TEN

Healing Foods

A healthy diet increases your energy, but will also benefit your mind and body in other ways. Eating poorly or the wrong kind of food causes stress, which results in a loss of vitality and can lead to ill health, both mentally and physically. The modern diet typically has a massive emphasis on rich and fat-filled foods, leading to obesity, bloating, bowel disorders, aching joints, lack of concentration, depression, and fatigue.

Balance and moderation is important—a healthy diet contains a small proportion of rich foods, but the bulk of it should be made up of vegetables, fruit, grains, and carbohydrates. The modern diet often includes foods that encourage the growth of *candida albicans*—a yeast that is present normally in the gut, but which causes fatigue, headaches, and bloating if it grows out of control. Changing what you eat can bring things back under control again. A diet can also be used to boost the immune system and cut down the effects of toxins from the environment. Some foods can actually remove toxins from our bodies and can be used to detoxify the system and soak up free radicals.

Candida albicans is encouraged to grow out of control if you eat too much sugar, the saturated fats in dairy products, and red meat, alcohol, vinegar, and blue cheese.

Replace these foods with fresh fruit, vegetables—especially dark-green leafy vegetables—whole grains, fresh nuts, squash, and sesame seeds.

Free radicals are short-lived and destructive molecules that are made by the body. They can impair the lining of the arteries, cause internal inflammation, and lead to premature aging. The body's natural defenses against free radicals rely on sufficient levels of vitamins A, C, and E and the minerals selenium and zinc.

We are surrounded by toxins in modern life—fumes from traffic, CFCs from air-conditioning systems, refrigerators, and aerosol sprays, and various metals in some common household products such as toothpaste. Heavy metals can be removed from the body by foods that contain substances that bind to the metal and encourage elimination.

TO REMOVE MERCURY, EAT FOODS RICH IN:

Calcium—dark-green vegetables, fresh seeds, milk

Zinc—almonds, carrots, cauliflower, chicken,

cucumber, egg yolks, oats, oysters, sardines, sesame and

sunflower seeds

TO REMOVE LEAD, EAT FOODS RICH IN:

Pectin—apples

Algin—seaweed

Vitamin C—strawberries, citrus fruit,
kiwifruit, potatoes

Fiber—fruit, vegetables, and whole grains

Zinc—almonds, carrots, cauliflower, chicken,
cucumber, egg yolks, oats, oysters, sardines,
sesame and sunflower seeds

TO REMOVE ALUMINUM, EAT FOODS RICH IN:

Iron—nuts, seeds, whole-grain products

Zinc—almonds, carrots, cauliflower, chicken, cucumber, egg yolks, oats, oysters, sardines, sesame and sunflower seeds

Detoxify

The liver processes toxins, but it can become overloaded.
There are several things that you can incorporate into your
diet to support and detoxify your liver.

Drink at least 8 cups of water each day.

Foods for optimum liver function

Apples

Apricots

Bananas

Blueberries

Figs

Kiwifruit

Pears

Asparagus

Beets

Carrots

Chickpeas

Onions

Squash

Sweet potatoes

Buckwheat	Chicken
Flaxseed	Eggs
Millet	Salmon
Oats	Soy
Rye	
Whole wheat	

Cooking substantially reduces B vitamins
and vitamin C and breaks down the fiber in
vegetables. Ensure that your diet contains plenty
of raw fruit and vegetables.

Foods to reduce stress

FOODS RICH IN MAGNESIUM

Almonds

Cod

Dark-green leafy vegetables

Nuts

Soy

FOODS RICH IN VITAMIN C

Cauliflower

Citrus fruit

Mango

Papaya

Potatoes

Strawberries

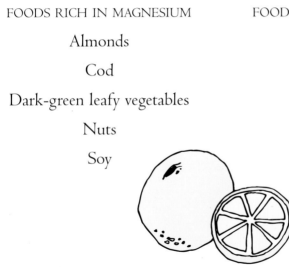

Mood foods

Sugar is a fuel that the body can easily turn into energy, but when you eat foods that release their sugar too quickly, your blood sugar will rise sharply. This triggers the production of insulin—which will bring the body's sugar levels down again fast. High blood sugar makes you feel full of energy, while low blood sugar makes you feel lethargic, tense, and depressed.

To get a consistent energy release and keep your mood on an even keel, combine complex carbohydrates with fiber and protein at each meal or snack.

Make sure you eat before you are really hungry to avoid your blood-sugar levels from dropping too low.

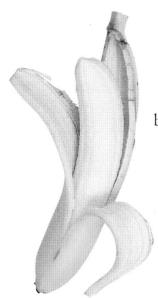

Low levels of dopamine have
been linked to anxiety and depression—
eat bananas, cottage cheese, herrings,
and sesame and pumpkin seeds to
prevent your levels from dropping.

Depression is also linked to low levels of B vitamins,
so increase your intake of foods rich in B vitamins:

BI

THIAMIN

Brewer's yeast, brown rice,
soy, wheat germ

B3

NIACIN

Brewer's yeast, chicken,
eggs, fish

B12

CYANOCOBALAMIN

Dairy products, fish, spirulina

(blue-green algae)

B9

FOLIC ACID

Brown rice, calves' liver, eggs,

green leafy vegetables, soy

CHAPTER ELEVEN

Affirmations

If we continually feed ourselves negative thoughts, negative things will happen. Therefore if we can feed ourselves positive thoughts, it will lead to a positive outcome. This is the basis on which affirmations operate.

Affirmation is the process of continually building yourself up by making positive and life-affirming statements to yourself. As small children we believe what adults tell us—if you are constantly told you are good and smart, you will tend to be that way and will continue to tell yourself the same thing as you grow up. However, if you are criticized, you can grow up overly critical of yourself, constantly putting yourself down and making demeaning statements. This does not mean that it is all your parents' fault—as a child you may have misunderstood the meaning of what they said—and even if you didn't, as you grow into an adult you no longer have to agree with them.

Affirmations really do work—not instantly, but over time. As well as putting positive feedback into your life, they also teach you to love yourself and to forgive yourself for past mistakes.

Working with a mirror is one of the most effective ways to get fast results with affirmations. As children, we probably received negative messages from people standing in front of us and looking us in the eye. If you stand in front of a mirror and look yourself in the eye, the message you give yourself goes straight to your subconscious, down a tried and tested route.

Look deep into your own eyes in the mirror
and say your affirmations out loud.

Positive affirmations fill the space and leave
no room for *negative* phrases.
Repeating positive statements prevents your mind from
running on fruitlessly with pointless *thoughts*

Work out one or two affirmations to improve your life. Write them down ten or twenty times during the day. Every time you pass a mirror, say them to yourself. Say them to yourself when you first wake up and just before you go to sleep.

DAILY AFFIRMATIONS
I love myself.
This is one of the best days of my life.
All is well.

SELF-HEALING AFFIRMATIONS

I am now taking full responsibility for my thoughts, emotions, and actions.
I have space in my life for the things I cherish.
I am healthy and I love my body.

EMOTIONAL AFFIRMATIONS

I am joyous and happy.
I am filled with love and affection.
I am relaxed.
I am safe and I trust the process of life.

LIFE AFFIRMATIONS

I have a wonderful life.

I am open to finding a wonderful new place to live.

I deserve the best and I accept it now.

I will savor every moment as a great opportunity.

WORK AFFIRMATIONS

I am deeply fulfilled by all that I do.
I trust my own judgment.
I am well organized.
I get along well with those I work with.
I will take action—even if that action is an intentional
decision to do nothing.
I am open to finding a wonderful new job.

SUCCESS AFFIRMATIONS

I am prosperous and successful.

Everything I touch is a success.

Wonderful opportunities are everywhere for me.

There are plenty of clients for my services.

"Waking up each morning feeling happy sends positive signals. Beginning the day as though a black cloud were hovering over you produces a negative effect."

Uri Geller *Mind Medicine*

LIMITING THOUGHTS

Negative, defensive thinking is approaching the subject

from the wrong direction.

Don't think "I hate my job."

Think "I am ready to find a wonderful new job."

Write down all your negative thoughts as they occur to you, and find ways in which they can be turned around to become positive.

Be careful how you phrase your affirmation. If you say
to yourself, "I will now meet the man of my dreams," he
may be what you dreamed of—but he may also turn out to
live hundreds of miles away or already be married!
Instead, say something more like, "I am ready to have a wonderful
new relationship that will make me very happy."

Don't say, "I am going to be happy," as that is setting it in the future. Say "I am happy," which puts it in the present— something that is happening right now.

CHAPTER TWELVE

Exercise to Harmonize
Body and Soul

Exercise is one of the best things you can do to relieve stress—and it also keeps your body fit at the same time. Any kind of physical exertion counts as exercise—including yoga, cycling, walking, and dancing. The most important thing is to choose something you enjoy, or you will not keep to a regime.

Some forms of exercise are particularly beneficial to both mind and body. Tai chi has been practiced in China since ancient times and has become very popular in the West for its effect on physical and mental well-being. Tai chi began as a combative exercise to develop fluid power as a form of martial art, but developed into an exercise to improve the health.

Pilates was originally created as an exercise for injured dancers. It works on the basis of correcting the body's alignment so that you learn to move gracefully while working on your muscles. Because of its emphasis on alignment, this is a form of exercise that should be done with a teacher, rather than alone.

The correct amount of physical exercise varies from person to person—do not try to do too much at once if you have not done significant exercise for some time.

Exercise does not have to be strenuous or tied to the gym or a workout studio. If you choose something you really enjoy, you are more likely to keep it up.

There are three basic types of exercise—weight bearing, which is anything involving weights, aerobic, and nonaerobic.

Aerobic exercise raises the heart rate, increases oxygen intake, and removes waste products faster. However, it also increases free radical production, so a higher intake of antioxidants will be needed.

Aerobics

Cycling

Rowing

Running

Swimming

Walking

Nonaerobic exercise stretches muscles and tones the body, and is much more gentle than aerobic.

Ballet

Pilates

Stretching

Tai chi

Yoga

"A bear, however hard he tries, grows tubby without exercise."

Pooh's Little Instruction Book

Daily exercise can significantly lower your chances of developing heart disease.

It is never too late to start exercising—even people in their fifties who have never undertaken any significant physical activity and already have heart problems will cut their risk of having a heart attack by starting moderate exercise.

Adequate physical exercise will also increase your tolerance to social, emotional, and chemical stress.

"Too many people confine their exercise to jumping to conclusions, running up bills, stretching the truth, bending over backward, lying down on the job, sidestepping responsibility, and pushing their luck."

Author unknown

There are several different types of yoga—hatha and raja yoga concentrate on the body and mental control, karma yoga is connected with action, and bahakta yoga is based on devotion. Hatha yoga is the kind most commonly practiced in the West. Through physical exercises, breathing exercises, and relaxation techniques, the practice of yoga will cleanse the body, calm the mind, and bring you back into perfect balance.

The philosophy of hatha yoga is that the body is precious. As a starting point it encourages good posture, and many of the exercises are designed to improve the condition and suppleness of the spine. Practiced regularly, yoga will bring increased mobility, toned and strengthened muscles, a sense of well-being, a focused mind, and the ability to relax quickly and effectively.

When adults move, it is often in a disjointed and exaggerated way, because each set of muscles is controlled by your emotional state, sudden thoughts, and reactions conditioned by years of habit. Tai chi aims to correct this and return to the pliability and fluidness of childhood by learning to move the body as a unit. Tai chi basically consists of a number of postures, which are connected together by moving fluidly and slowly in a continuous chain of movement.

Part of the concept of tai chi is to assist your invisible life energy, or chi, to flow correctly around the body, clearing blockages and stagnant areas and slowing overactive chi.

To study tai chi properly you will need to find a teacher.

Practiced regularly, tai chi tones muscles, reduces stress, and improves your blood flow, energy levels, and breathing.

Pilates was originally created as an exercise for injured dancers, but it can teach you correct body alignment so that you learn to move gracefully while working on your muscles. It increases strength and flexibility and improves posture. Nothing is forced or repetitive.

To learn Pilates correctly, you must either attend classes
or have private lessons—since correct body alignment is
an important factor, expert teaching is essential.
Learning Pilates is a long-term process—it will take time to
master it correctly and for all its benefits to become apparent.

"The sovereign invigorator of the body is exercise, and of all the exercises walking is the best."

Thomas Jefferson

350

CHAPTER THIRTEEN

A Good Night's Sleep

About one third of our life is spent sleeping and it is vitally important to our health and well-being that we get a good night's sleep. Refusing to allow sleep is a form of torture that has been used successfully to break the spirit of prisoners. Enough sleep is difficult to quantify, as it is not the same for everyone. Some people seem to manage on less than six hours a night, others need more than nine—but a healthy average is around seven to eight hours.

We sleep to replenish our energy levels and to allow our bodies time to relax and recover from the stresses of the day. If you start feeling the need to sleep for long periods, your body may be telling you that you are depleting your reserves too much and need more rest. It is also important to get extra sleep when you have been ill, to allow the body to build itself up again.

To get the greatest benefit from sleep, it is important to be comfortable, with your body relaxed. Problems getting to sleep can be alleviated by following a few rules and doing exercises to help you relax before bed. It may also help not to try and take all your sleep in one batch—a daytime nap can be very beneficial.

Some tips to try if you have difficulty getting to sleep at night

Establish a bedtime routine—the repetition of familiar actions will signal your body that it is time to begin winding down to go to sleep.

Gentle exercise, such as taking a short walk after your evening meal, will aid your digestion, but do not get involved in heavy exercise too close to bedtime.

Avoid stimulants, such as coffee, cigarettes, and alcohol, late at night just before you go to bed. They will interfere with the winding-down process. Alcohol may temporarily "knock you out" but you will probably wake up several times during the night.

Find something soothing and relaxing to do for the hour before you go to bed, such as listening to music, having a relaxing bath, or enjoying a hot, milky drink.

Practice your favorite relaxation *technique, such as meditation, massage, or deep breathing, just before you go to bed.*

Make sure there is fresh air in the bedroom,
do not smoke in there, and try to keep one window
at least partly open.

The bedroom temperature should be set at around 60–65°F. Make sure your bed is comfortable and that the room is sufficiently dark—light is a natural cue for waking. Try to eliminate background noise or mask it with relaxing music.

*"Life is something that happens when
you can't get to sleep."*

Fran Lebowitz

If you still feel wide awake, don't lie there worrying that you cannot sleep. Listen to music or read a magazine— make sure it is something relaxing and nonstimulating, or you will never get to sleep.

Don't worry too much about how many hours of sleep you are getting—everybody needs different amounts to function efficiently. If you are not feeling any ill effects, you are probably getting enough.

Dreams are an important part of a good night's sleep. They mirror the sleeper's recent waking experiences, but often combine them with unresolved conflicts and emotions. Dreams both release inner tensions and can alert us to a problem—the unconscious mind can pinpoint topics that our conscious mind has overlooked or refuses to acknowledge.

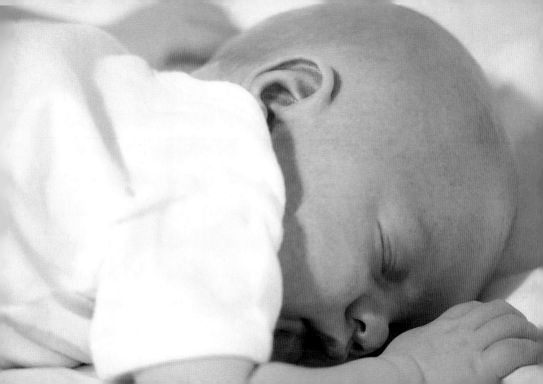

"Dreams are today's answers to tomorrow's questions."

Edgar Cayce

CHAPTER FOURTEEN

Homeopathic Remedies

Homeopathy works on the principle that "like cures like" and that the body should be encouraged to deal with any problems itself. It is a successful alternative to conventional medicine for those who are wary of taking too many manufactured drugs and would like to follow a more natural way of life. It works with your body's healing processes, rather than overriding them. Used correctly, it is even safe for pregnant mothers, babies, and elderly people.

One of the basic tenets of homeopathy is that it treats the whole person, not just the symptoms. It has many remedies to maintain and promote good health, but to work at their best, these should be used in conjunction with changes in diet and lifestyle. Some homeopathic remedies are also widely used in conventional medicine, but if you take them as a "quick-fix" remedy, although they may work in a limited way, you are not taking them homeopathically.

At its deepest level, homeopathic medicine is preventive—it encourages the immune system to respond and improves your mental and emotional state so that everything works smoothly to keep illness at bay.

Store homeopathic medicines in a cool, dark place. Keep the tops well screwed on and do not place them next to items with a strong odor. If they are stored correctly, homeopathic remedies remain potent for up to a hundred years.

When taking homeopathic remedies, avoid coffee, alcohol, tobacco, minty flavorings, highly perfumed toiletries, and the essential oils used in aromatherapy. These all have the ability to counteract homeopathic medicines.

Homeopathic remedies can be bought from health-food stores and from some pharmacists. They usually come as a pill and in a potency of 6c—although sometimes 30c is available. For most applications, 6c potency is fine, but for chronic or severe symptoms, 30c should be used.

To take the remedy, tip one pill from the bottle into the bottle top, and from there drop it under the tongue and allow it to dissolve. Try to avoid touching the pill with your fingers.

The pills are usually made of lactose, so if you are allergic to lactose, it is possible to buy remedies in solution in a bottle with a dropper. Put one or two drops under the tongue.

Top ten homeopathic remedies for stress:
Take four times daily for up to seven days.

ACONITE

From *Aconitum napellus*

Used to relieve states of acute
stress or chronic tension

ARNICA

From *Arnica montana*

Used to minimize the effects of
shock and insomnia

ARSENICUM

From *Arsenicum album*

Used to treat restless

anxiety and fear

HYPERICUM

From *Hypericum perforatum*

Used to treat the nervous

system and depression

IGNATIA

From *Ignatia amara*

Used to treat rapid changes
of mood, fear, and inability
to work

NATRUM SULPHATE

From *Sodium sulphate*

Used to treat anxiety and anger

NUX	PHOSPHORUS
From *Nux vomica*	From *Amorphous phosphorus*
Used to treat anxiety, anger, frustration, and weariness	Used to treat nervous tension

SULPHUR

From flowers of sulphur

Used to treat lack of energy
and willpower

TARENTULA

From *Lycosa tarentula*

Used to treat sudden mood
changes, restlessness, and
tormented behavior

Flower essences are body-mind-spirit remedies,
which can help you relax and deal with stress and change.
They can take some time to take effect, but changes
can be quite dramatic.

The normal dosage of flower essence is to take three or four drops under your tongue, two to four times per day. At the start of the course, it may be beneficial to take the drops six to eight times a day for the first few days before reducing the dose.

You can also add flower essences to bath water, drinks, or in spray bottles.

Flower essences are nonaddictive and completely safe.

ASPEN

Populus tremula

Helps to soothe anxiety

and fear

BLUE VERVAIN

Verbena hastata

Induces peaceful rest

and sweet calm

BORAGE

Borago officinalis

Relieves sorrow and depression

CHAMOMILE

Matricaria recutita

Supports the development of

peace and calm

CLARY SAGE

Salvia sclarea

Helps to clear blockages in your
life and allow you to progress

DEVIL'S CLUB

Oplopanax horridus

Provides comfort during
periods when your energy
is at a low ebb

ECHINACEA

Echinacea purpurea

Helps you to let go of your
outmoded self-image and
supports you as you move on to
a new way of life

IMPATIENS

Impatiens

Helps the development
of patience

LAVENDER

Lavandula officinalis

Aids relaxation and helps
you find a new purpose
in life

OLIVE

Olea europaea

Eases mental and physical
exhaustion

TRICOLOR SAGE

Salvia officinalis

Brings love into your

daily life

RESCUE REMEDY

A first-aid treatment to reduce

trauma and ease stress

WHITE CHESTNUT

Aesculus hippocastanum

Aids relaxation and helps

you find a new purpose

in life

WILD ROSE

Rosa canina

Helps to clear resignation and

apathy, leading to increased

vitality and the ability to make

life meaningful